Cornerstone Collector's Guide to

GLASS

BY

Jeffrey Weiss

CORNERSTONE LIBRARY
Published by Simon & Schuster
NEW YORK

Text by Susan Osborn
Designed by Deborah Bracken
Photographers: Michael Kanouff,
David Leach, Jeffrey Weiss
Acknowledgements:
JOHNNY JUPITER
PHASES, 163 Eighth Avenue,
New York, New York 10016
Bob Perzel, POPKORN
Walter Hazzard, Robert Tankesley,
TOPEDO CORPORATION, 94 Christopher Street,
New York, New York

Manufactured in the United States of America
10 9 8 7 6 5 4 3 2 1
Library of Congress Catalog Number: 80-70713

ISBN 0-346-12534-0

TABLE OF CONTENTS

Introduction

F ew hobbies have become as quickly popular as the collecting of the inexpensive, machine-made colored glassware manufactured in America between the middle of the 1920s and the early 1940s. Depression glassware clubs and organizations have appeared all over the country and shows are now regularly scheduled local events. Partly because of nostalgia and partly because of their cheery colors, Depression glassware has become one of the most sought-after collectibles.

Depression glassware is the unmistakable representative of an era. The wealthy and the fashion-conscious were the first to dress their tables in glass dishes of amethyst, ruby and emerald. The mass-produced glass symbolized the modern industrial age, and as such was considered the ultimate chic. But in the years following the Great Crash, cost — not style — dictated fashion, and everyone, rich and poor, used Depression glass. Flawed and poorly finished as it was, Depression glass could be purchased for a few pennies at the five-and-ten-cent store, and it added a touch of color to the lives of those who suffered through those lean years.

Glass manufacturers used color to help conceal impurities in the glass.

The
Real Thing

The colored glassware that we now call Depression glass was made primarily during the years between 1928 or 1929 through the 1930s and a year or two into the 1940s. The term Depression glass does not include all of the glass made in America during those years though. Not all glass companies of the era made Depression glass. For example, Fostoria, Heisey, Westmoreland and Cambridge all made some Depression glass, but not all of their wares were machine-made or mass-produced. Even when made in the same colors, better-quality glass is not considered Depression glass. Orthodox collectors define Depression glass as *glass tableware and giftware, primarily machine-*

made, that was originally inexpensive or even free. The glass was distributed nationally and only rarely was a piece worked or decorated by hand.

Depression glass was produced in more than 25 colors, usually transparent hues of amber, blue, green, pink, red and yellow. Much of it was made without color and called crystal, and many patterns were made in translucent or opaque shades. Most collectors refer to the color by the manufacturers' trade names (see Color Glossary). Color as well as pattern and shape affect the value of a piece. Few pieces were made in light blue, dark blue or ruby red, and even fewer in smoke.

After the Great Crash, glassware skyrocketed in popularity. It was inexpensive to produce; even the cheapest earthenware was more expensive than glass. Glass plates were high fashion during

Brightly-colored kitchenware makes an attractive still-life.

the late '20s, and to people who survived the Crash, glass tableware looked expensive and stylish. Furthermore, glass could be molded into other items that anyone would need and use, and manufacturers made pieces in a wide variety of shapes and colors. Advertisers, recognizing the popularity of the glass, knew it could be used as a premium to enhance the sales of their clients' products.

By 1925, the glassmaking industry was almost entirely mechanized. Glassblowing artisans were no longer needed to make bottles and jars. By the late '20s, glass companies were set up to produce huge quantities of inexpensive tableware, cookware and kitchen items.

Most Depression glass was machine-molded and produced automatically by forcing liquid glass through pipes into pressing molds. The technique and the machinery were new in the '20s, but abandoned by the late '30s in favor of

Depression glass of many colors, makes an eye-catching display on a window sill.

Octagonal dishes of every kind were popular during the Depression.

even more advanced molding methods. With the newer machinery, manufacturers could produce decorative glassware that had an etched appearance but did not require any handiwork: the design or pattern was actually cut into the mold. The glass was of the cheapest commercial quality ("bottle glass") and the finished piece showed many bubbles and flaws. Manufacturers used color and pattern to help conceal the impurities in the glass.

The primary reason for the immediate popularity of the glass was its price. Individual pieces sold for less than a nickel. Housewives could collect whole sets free as glassware was used as giveaways or premiums. Cinemas offered "Dish Night," when, for the price of admission, a Fred Astaire fan could see two movies and walk home with a set of glasses or a luncheon set.

9

Besides tableware, every manufacturer made kitchen items. Glass factories poured out syrup pitchers, measuring cups, reamers, salt and pepper sets, berry bowls, butter dishes, spice shakers, mixing bowls and cruets. Because most of the kitchen items saw constant use and the quality of the glass was poor, only a few pieces have survived, and they sell for very high prices.

Because kitchenware saw constant use and often broke, measuring cups like this one are highly prized by today's collectors.

Manufacturers promoted their products with cruets, reamers, and sugar and creamer sets.

Complete sets of any pattern, in any color are very rare and highly desirable.

How the Glass Was Made

Depression glass was made of silica (sand), soda ash and limestome. It contained no expensive ingredients. (Some companies did make better-quality tableware and accessory pieces by adding lead to the molten material or by hand-finishing a piece, but this is not considered true Depression glass, even though it was produced in quantity and often in shapes and patterns similar to the cheaper glassware.) The ingredients were melted or fused together in a ceramic tank and the liquid glass poured into pipes which were connected to automatic pressing molds. The mass-production of tank glass (as it is called) was an innovation process that allowed large quantities of glassware to be turned out in a single operation.

Color

Manufacturers used color to cover the flaws and imperfections in the glassware. Natural glass colors, produced by impurities in the raw material, are amber, olive-amber, olive-green and aqua. Other colors can be made by adding various metal oxides to the raw ingredients in the basic glass mixture. The end color depends on the amount of oxide added, the impurities in the basic glass mixture, the temperature, and the amount of time needed to make the piece. Glass can be made in almost any color, but some colors are more expensive to produce than others. Red is relatively expensive because it requires the addition of copper, selenium or gold. Green and yellow, on the other hand, are relatively inexpensive, and a lot of glass was made in various shades of these two colors.

Pink color of this classically-shaped pitcher is the stamp of the 1930s.

Pattern

Patterns were designed to accommodate the flawed, mass-produced glass. Intricate designs served the manufacturers in the same way as color: they helped conceal imperfections in the glass. Besides, the more elaborately patterned the glass, the less likely it was to show scratches from knives and forks. One of the most successful patterns of the time was one in which the rough texture of tree bark was reproduced on the surface of the glass.

Pattern designers drew from a wealth of traditional American glass patterns. Many patterns were derived from the traditional Sandwich glass patterns, popular during the 19th century. Designers also adapted the old designs of many-faceted glassware. Traditional geometric patterns were made without mold-etched designs, but the many surfaces caught the light and created an effect similar to that of expensive cut glass. Collectors of both Depression glass and traditional glassware should know, though, that while few designs were literally copied, many of the pattern names are identical.

Many new modernistic patterns were created to appeal to the '30s sensibility; patterns were derived from the decorative art styles popular during the time. For example, the Jeannette Glass Company made an innovative pattern called "Sierra," a geometric, flashy pinwheel shape — an Art Deco derivative. While this pattern was considered very modern, it did not sell well because its serrated edges chipped easily. "Tea Room," another geometric, decorative pattern by the Indiana Glass Company, was more successful. "Moderntone," a simple but elegant pattern by the Hazel Atlas Glass Company, epitomized the best in modern design of the glassware of the era. Other patterns, like "Sharon" by the Federal

13

Glass Company, incorporated the asymmetry of Art Nouveau, and patterns like "Iris" and "Floral" by the Jeannette Glass Company used flora and fauna motifs popular during the first years of the 20th century. Many patterns combined traditional and modern motifs. "Queen Mary" by the Hocking Glass Company is classically shaped with vertical ribs, but the pattern assumes a decidedly '30s look when colored pink. "Cubist," a pattern by Jeannette, is an adaptation of a glass pattern from the earliest days of American glassmaking, but the company gave it an up-to-date name to appeal to a more modern sensibility. Likewise, many new patterns were given names that would appeal to traditionalists. For example, Hocking called a modern pattern "Colonial" in the hope of appealing to those who knew of the similar, earlier "Knife and Fork" pattern.

Shape

The shape of a piece of glass is as important as color and pattern in determining its value. Dinner plates are expensive, as are complete sugar and

Matching creamer and sugar sets are rare.

Sandwich servers that still have their handles are extremely valuable.

creamer and salt and pepper sets. A covered dish such as a butter dish with its original dome is very expensive. A sandwich server with a handle in the center or any footed piece is also very expensive.

Many of the shapes of Depression glass were determined by changes in American eating habits — changes which resulted from dramatic changes in food production methods following World War I. Designers fashioned dishes which would be appropriate for serving the new products. For example, ice cream had become readily available, and new glass dishes were needed to

15

serve ice cream sodas, banana splits and sundaes. In fact, soda fountain glassware of the '30s is one of the most popular categories with collectors.

After World War I, scientists began studying nutrition, and compartmented grill plates resulted from the wave of information about the well-balanced diet.

During the Depression, many cinemas offered a free set of dishes, for the price of admission.

With the repeal of Prohibition in 1933, manufacturers made all shapes and sizes of glassware for the huge variety of "new" alcoholic beverages. The "Sportsman Series" by the Hazel Atlas Company is currently one of the most desirable Depression glass cocktail sets.

By the middle of the '30s, many families had automatic refrigerators and glass manufacturers began producing refrigerator ware. These pieces were designed to store food with the most economical use of the limited interior space of the new refrigerators. Most containers were oblong or square and many were designed to stack one on top of another to save space. The containers were lightweight and well suited for the smaller amounts of food kept in a refrigerator. Most refrigerator ware was made in green, amber, blue, opaque green, white, light blue and cream, and many pieces were embossed with geometric patterns, ivy leaves or vegetables.

To make the most economical use of the limited space in the new refrigerator, storage containers like these were designed to stack one on top of another.

Manufacturers used elaborate patterns to hide defects in the glass.

Geometric designs like these were extremely popular during the 1930s.

A complete sugar and creamer set is prized by collectors.

Simple but elegant glassware represents the best of the modern design of the Depression.

Some shapes were adapted from popular ceramic patterns. Wide-rimmed ceramic plates were fashionable during the early '20s so wide-rimmed glass plates were produced in the '30s. Other shapes, like many of the new patterns, derived from the geometric art popular at the time. For example, square dishes were very fashionable during the '30s and patterns like "Adam," "Princess," "Lorain" and "Sylvan" were bestsellers. In general, though, most of the tableware shapes were small and simple. Few people could afford enormous roasts or fowl so few manufacturers made oversized vegetable dishes or meat platters.

Merchandising the New Glass

Colored glassware was pretty, useful, plentiful and, most important, cheap. S. S. Kresge, Sears and Roebuck and other department stores sold a set of four five-piece place setting for as little as $1.99. "Glass is Correct!" read the Sears advertisements.

Depression glass was made in a countless variety of shapes and patterns.

Almost everyone could afford to have the dinner table set with completely coordinated glassware, for almost every imaginable piece — salad plates, beverage sets, sugar and creamer sets, butter dishes, candy dishes, soup bowls, dinner plates, salt and pepper sets — were made in matching colors and patterns. Magazines showed pictures of gracious living and decorating with glass. In an article titled "Serve It in Colored Glassware" in the September 1929 issue of *Better Homes and Gardens*, a writer described the "aristocracy" of colored glass. The writer suggested that the housewife choose the color of the glassware to be used that night to coordinate with her dinner dress and admonished, "Whatever it is, serve it in glass!" Housewives wanted to imitate what they saw in the pictures, and those who couldn't afford Fostoria, could always find a less expensive substitute in the Sears and Roebuck catalogue.

Colored glassware was used to promote furniture stores, theaters, appliance stores, gas stations and food companies. Glassware helped the distributor sell his product during hard times: it cost him little but it looked like a lot to the customer. A manufacturer could print the name of his product on an item and give it away or sell it as a bargain.

A patterned pitcher enhances any decorating scheme.

Almost every kind of company found some promotional use for glass measuring cups, shot glasses, tumblers, plates, pitchers and bowls. Soft drink companies distributed mugs and glasses, soap companies gave away dispensers and dishes, spice companies handed out shakers. Refrigerator manufacturers sold refrigerators fully equipped with lightweight, "stackable" glass containers. Fruit companies promoted their products with reamers, vinegar companies gave away cruets, and furniture distributors offered a free set of dishes to customers who purchased a bedroom or living room set.

One of the most popular promotions was an ashtray with a removable miniature tire around the rim. The name of the tire distributor was usually embossed on the glass or printed on a paper decal attached to the underside. These promotions were discontinued at the beginning of World War II, due to the acute rubber shortage, and are very desirable today.

With the advent of radio, advertisers could reach every town in the country, and food manufacturers turned their products into national fads. For example, Jell-O was advertised nationwide and glass manufacturers produced stemmed dessert dishes that became the "last word" in serving the new dessert. To entice consumers, General Mills packed the eminently popular Shirley Temple glassware — which included a cobalt milk pitcher, cereal bowl and mug, each with a photographic image of the child movie star — into cereal packages. After the 1920s and the development of the refrigerated box car, citrus growers launched a huge advertising campaign to promote the consumption of their product. The Sunkist Orange Company of California offered a glass reamer (made by the McKee Glass Company) with Sunkist embossed on it for 50 cents.

Fruit companies often promoted their products with reamers.

Their pretty colors are one reason why depression glass has regained popularity in recent years.

23

Where to Find Depression Glass

Some kinds of Depression glass are easier to find and more affordable than others. Selecting the type of glass you want to collect is partly a matter of taste. Before you begin collecting, know what you are looking for. If you are just starting to collect, you may want to go to a glass show to examine the different kinds of glassware available. There you can find out which patterns, colors, and shapes appeal to you. Glass shows are also good places to establish the current value of various patterns. There are over 200 Depression glass clubs in the United States, many of which sponsor annual shows. Some of these shows are huge; dealers exhibit between 20,000 and 50,000 pieces of glass. If you do not find the pattern you are interested in, ask the dealer if he has it.

During the Depression, this cup and saucer set probably
sold for a dime; today they're worth $3.50.

Table sets included every conceivable piece: cookie jars,
relish plates, preserve dishes, salad plates, beverage sets,
sugar and creamer sets, dinner plates, butter dishes, cups
and saucers, and salt and pepper sets. Complete sets are
rare.

DEPRESSION GLASS SHOWS

Below is a list of some of the largest regularly scheduled Depression glass shows in the country.

January	Sanford, FL
	San Jose, CA
February	Houston, TX
	Miami, FL
	New Orleans, LA
	Sacramento, CA
March	Charlotte, NC
March/April	Greenbelt, MD
	Southington, CT
April	Denver, CO
	Pittsburgh, PA
	St. Louis, MO
	Springfield, IL
May	Anaheim, CA
	Rochester, MI
June	San Jose, CA
July	Marietta, GA
August	Pensacola, FL
	Sacramento, CA
September	Lakeland, FL
	New Orleans, LA
October	Cleveland, OH
	Marietta, GA
	Milwaukee, WI
	Ypsilanti, MI
November	Anaheim, CA
	Cincinnati, OH
	St. Louis, MO

FOR MORE INFORMATION:

The clubs and publications listed below have information on glassware shows across the country.

National Depression Glass
   Association
News & Views
721 Cambridge Dr.
Lees Summit, MO 64063

Paden City Partyline
13325 Danvers Way
Westminster, CA 92683

Glass Review
P.O. Box 2315
Costa Mesa, CA 92626

National Glass, Pottery & Collectibles
Journal
361 Main St.
Kutztown, PA 19530

Obsession in Depression
20415 Harvest Ave.
Lakewood, CA 90715

Depression Glass National Market
Appraisal Report
2943 Realty Court
Gastonia, NC 28016

Diamond patterned relish dishes like this one are very popular with today's collectors.

Flea markets, auctions and back-yard sales are likely places to find depression glass.

There is a glassware category for every price range. There are plenty of patterns in a wide range of colors readily available to the collector with limited funds. If money is not a problem, most experts advise you to collect a more expensive pattern. The more expensive patterns are most desirable and are therefore in greatest demand. The market value of expensive patterns is stable, but will most likely increase over the years. That means that a pattern that is initially more expensive will have a better resale value. But a collector need not limit himself to one particular style or pattern. You might want to collect in bits and pieces and buy one platter, a couple of cookie jars and a few salt and pepper shakers.

Whatever you decide to collect, you should familiarize yourself with a range of patterns and styles. You should know for example, that dealers in different areas of the country have different names for the same pattern. "Cherry Blossom" by Jeannette is also called "Cherry," "Cherry Spray," "Panelled Cherry," and "Banded Cherry." The more you know, the less likely you are to be cheated or misled. Also, if you are familiar with a wide range of patterns and styles, you might just land yourself a bargain. Imagine stumbling upon a piece priced at $5 which you know is worth $50!

If you really dig around, you can make a collection with little more than time and energy. The first place to look for Depression glass is **your own basement**, garage or attic. Everyone used Depression glass, and almost everyone still has a few pieces around the house.

Check your local newspaper for **garage sales**, tag sales or yard sales, or any other kind of household sale where people might be selling glassware they have found in their attics or basements. Often, these people are anxious to get rid of their old glass and will sell it for a very small sum. You can usually find a decent supply of glassware at bargain prices at church bazaars or rummage sales.

Second-hand shops like thrift shops and Salvation Army stores usually have regularly replenished supplies of glassware. If there is a second-hand shop near you, make a point of walking by the window at least once a week to examine new arrivals. Find out when the shopkeeper expects his next shipment, and be there when it arrives. That way, you'll have first choice.

Antique shops frequently have a stock of Depression glass, but reputable dealers usually know what they are doing so don't expect to find bargains or less expensive patterns in antique shops.

Check your newspaper for local **estate auctions** — you might be able to bid for just that piece you need to complete part of your collection. A word of caution about auction buying, though: examine the glassware carefully before you bid. Check for chips, flaws or any sign of repair that would lower the value of the glass. To check for chips, run your finger over the areas of the piece that are most prone to chipping (such as handles, edges, rims). Any flake or chip lowers the value of the piece.

You will probably find the best stock of Depression glass at **flea markets**. Flea markets are held in almost every state on a regular basis.

Swirled candy jar, widely available.

Today this plate, once valued at $1.00, is worth thirty-five times that.

A rare piece of ebony Depression glass like this one is keenly sought by collectors.

Green Doric, made between 1935 and 1938, was one of Jeannette's most popular patterns.

31

MAJOR FLEA MARKETS

Below is a small list of some of the better-known flea markets held around the country. Check your local newspaper for exact time and location.

California: Pasadena, Rosebowl
(monthly)

Indiana: Indianapolis, Fairgrounds
(monthly)

Kentucky: Louisville, Fairgrounds
(monthly)

Massachusetts: Brimfield (May, July,
September)

Ohio: Hartville (every Monday)
Manesville (monthly)
Springfield (monthly)

Pennsylvania: Lancaster /Reading
area (many
weekly)

Texas: Canton (weekend of
first Monday of
month)

MORE FLEA MARKETS

For further listings of auctions and flea markets in the **Northwest**, check the following publications:

The Antique Trader Weekly
P.O. Box 1050
Dubuque, IA 52001

Collectors News
Box 156
Grundy Center, IA 50638

Native Arts/West
Box 31196
Billings, MT 59107

West Coast Peddler
P.O. Box 4489
Downey, CA 90241

For further listings of auctions and flea markets in the **Southwest**, check the following publications:

Antiques Magazine
551 Fifth Ave.
New York, NY 10017

The Antique Trader Weekly
P.O. Box 1050
Dubuque, IA 52001

Bay Area Collector
P.O. Box 1210
Fremont, CA 94538

Native Arts/West
Box 31196
Billings, MT 59107

West Coast Peddler
P.O. Box 4489
Downey, CA 90241

For further listings of auctions and flea markets in the **Middle West**, check the following publications:

Antique Monthly
P.O. Drawer 2
Tuscaloosa, AL 35402

Antiques Magazine
551 Fifth Ave.
New York, NY 10017

The Antique Trader Weekly
P.O. Box 1050
Dubuque, IA 52001

Collectors News
Box 156
Grundy Center, IA 50638

Ohio Antique Review
P.O. Box 538
Worthington, OH 43085

Spinning Wheel
Antiques & Early Crafts
American Antiques and Crafts Society
Fame Ave.
Hanover, PA 17331

Tri-State Trader
P.O. Box 90
Knightstown, IN 46148

For further listings of auctions and flea markets in the **Southeast**, check the following publications:

Antique Monthly
P.O. Drawer 2
Tuscaloosa, AL 35402

The Antique Trader Weekly
P.O. Box 1050
Dubuque, IA 52001

Antiques Magazine
551 Fifth Ave.
New York, NY 10017

The Antiques Press
Florida's Newspaper of Antiques &
Collectibles
P.O. Box 12047
St. Petersburg, FL 33733

Collectors News
Box 156
Grundy Center, IA 50638

Spinning Wheel
Antiques & Early Crafts
American Antiques and Crafts Society
Fame Ave.
Hanover, PA 17331

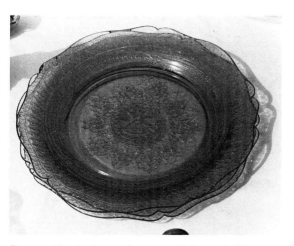

Pretty mold-etched plates like these added a touch of class to Depression tables.

Vertically ribbed fruit bowl, originally part of a set which included dinnerware, bon bon dishes, cruets, sandwich servers.

For further listings of auctions and flea markets in the **Mid-Atlantic** states, check the following publications:

Antique Monthly
P.O. Drawer 2
Tuscaloosa, AL 35402

Antiques Magazine
551 Fifth Ave.
New York, NY 10017

The Antique Trader Weekly
P.O. Box 1050
Dubuque, IA 52001

Collectors News
Box 156
Grundy Center, IA 50638

The New York-Pennsylvania Collector
Wolfe Publications, Inc.
4 South Main St.
Pittsford, NY 14534

Spinning Wheel
Antiques & Early Crafts
American Antiques and Crafts Society
Fame Ave.
Hanover, PA 17331

For further listings of auctions and flea markets in **New England**, check the following publications:

Antique Monthly
P.O. Drawer 2
Tuscallosa, AL 35402

The Antique Trader Weekly
P.O Box 1050
Dubuque, IA 52001

Antiques and the Arts Weekly
The Newtown Bee
Newtown, CT 06470

Antiques Magazine
551 Fifth Ave.
New York, NY 10017

Collectors News
Box 156
Grundy Center, IA 50638

Maine Antique Digest
Jefferson St.
Box 358
Waldoboro, ME 04572

Spinning Wheel
Antiques & Early Crafts
American Antiques and Crafts Society
Fame Ave.
Hanover, PA 17331

Crystal tea cups look especially gay when placed on colored place mats.

How to Buy

When collecting glass, the buyer must be wary. Reproductions and fakes are everywhere. The best protection against buying fakes or reproductions is to *know what you want to buy.* If you know the characteristics of the glass you are after, you will know if the dealer is trying to sell you something else. *Buy only from reputable dealers.* Reputable dealers will not represent or price a reproduction as an original, nor will they try to sell you a reproduction to which they have added scratches or other distress marks. Most reputable dealers will give you a detailed bill of sale or will offer you a "buy-back" guarantee.

Depression glass was manufactured in a rainbow of colors.

"Manhattan", made by Anchor Hocking between 1938-1941.

39

Complete Sets

Because depression glass was every-day-ware and saw constant use, complete sets are rare and very desirable.

Depression glass was everyday ware. It saw constant use. Most of it was not of very high quality, and some of it — like "Comet," a pattern manufactured during the '20s (probably by U.S. Glass) — was of very poor quality. The glass was thin and brittle and could not withstand extreme temperatures.

Because so much glassware was broken or lost, it is difficult today to find complete sets. During the 1930s, it was considered very stylish to set the table with a single pattern and color. Sets included *all* the pieces: candy dishes, cookie jars, fruit and dessert plates, preserves dishes, salt and pepper shakers, relish dishes, sandwich plates, butter dishes, dinner plates, cups and saucers. Today, collectors often pay as much for one plate as housewives did for an entire set. If you do manage to collect a complete set, it is sure to increase in value as Depression glass becomes more popular.

Individual pieces, often called occasional pieces or conversation pieces, were made and sold individually, not as part of a patterned set.

During the Depression this creamer and sugar set might have sold for 10¢.

Sherbets (center) once sold for less than $.50; today they're worth $2.25.

Price Guides

Prices of Depression glass vary from a few dollars to thousands of dollars, and for that reason, a price guide is an invaluable aid. The collectibles market has changed dramatically in the past two decades, and mass-marketing techniques are now applied to the selling of collectibles. A good price guide will indicate how much you should pay for a specific item and how much you should ask for if a dealer or another collector wants to buy it from you.

Prices vary and are subject to change depending upon geographical location, type of sale (auction, dealer, or yard sale) and time of year. A price guide will provide you with the information you need to stand up to a dealer, although you should remember that a price guide is just that — a guide. Prices do change every day. Don't be afraid to haggle with a dealer if his price seems too high. On the other hand, if a dealer quotes a price guide, don't be afraid to tell him that the color, condition or personal lack of appeal make you unwilling to pay the price quoted in his book. Weekly and monthly antiques magazines, as well as the classified section of you newspapers, are also good sources for current prices.

Condition and Value

Always try to buy the best you can afford. A good collection will increase in value over the years. The condition of the glass is the major determinant in the price of a piece. Repairs lessen the value of the glass. Because some repairs are difficult to detect among the intricate patterns, you should check the pieces carefully before you buy.

A piece in mint condition has no cracks, chips, repairs or ground-off edges. Glass that is not in mint condition, that is, glass that is cracked or scratched or poorly molded, will bring a small price if you try to resell it. Even if the piece is extremely rare, if it is not in mint condition, it will bring only a small amount of the price you would get if the glass were in perfect condition.

Flaws (bubbles and rough spots) in the glass do not mean that the glass is not worth collecting. Depression glass was made cheaply and the glass was produced with flaws. Flawed Depression glass is worth owning as long as it is otherwise in perfect condition.

Check patterned depression glass for chips and flaws before you buy.

Graceful vases attract the eyes of many collectors.

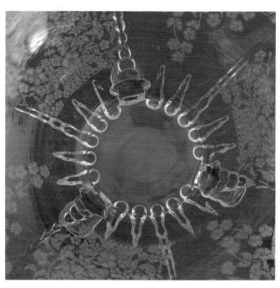

Colorless pieces like this cake plate were referred to by manufacturers as crystal.

Collectors should beware of reproductions: this Hobnail pitcher was rarely, if ever, made in blue.

Black was an uncommon Depression glass color and any piece is avidly sought by today's collectors.

45

Reselling Your Glass

This simple black vase adds a touch of elegance to any home.

If you choose to resell a piece, you will probably do best by selling to a reputable dealer. You can probably find a dealer who is interested in buying at the next Depression glass show in your area. If not, talk to people at your local Depression glass club. A member may want to buy and or may be able to put you in touch with a dealer who does. You can also find dealers' names in the ads in the weekly or monthly antiques magazines. Or you may find an interested dealer at a flea market.

The two key factors a dealer considers when buying are the popularity of and demand for that particular item. He will consider the popularity of both the color and the pattern with his potential buyers, and the amount of stock he already owns

46

The first place to look for depression glass is your own attic—you may find a stunning example like this.

in that particular style. His basic question will be: Can I make money on it? And, while a dealer will not pay you the going retail price for the piece, you should know what the item is worth.

If you are buying to resell, it is a good idea to catalogue your collection. Keep a record book or index of every piece of glass that you purchase (a loose-leaf notebook facilitates the addition or deletion of records). List the item, where and when it was obtained and any other information you feel is important. This kind of catalogue will help you evaluate the value and scope of your collection. You may even want to keep a record of the glass you no longer own in case you wish to refer to it in the future.

The Big Six

There were six major companies that manufactured most of the Depression glass collected today. Many smaller firms did not have the capital to set up a tank glass operation, and they could not compete with the larger companies.

Anchor Hocking

The Anchor Hocking Company of Lancaster, Ohio, produced a great number of collectible glassware patterns. Originally known as the Hocking Company, it merged with other companies in 1937 to form the Anchor Hocking Corporation. The firm was probably the largest manufacturer of

Depression tableware and therefore many of its patterns are still widely available.

Hocking kitchenware included salt and pepper shakers, sugar, tea and coffee containers, measuring cups, reamers, refrigerator ware, mixing bowls and tumblers. In 1929, Hocking made its first colored tank glassware, in green; in 1930, its first mold-etched pattern, "Cameo." During the '30s, the company made many yellow and pink patterns.

Unlike earthenware, glass can be molded into a wide variety of shapes.

Federal

The Federal Glass Company of Columbus, Ohio, began making green restaurant supplies, tumblers, kitchenware and tableware in the late '20s. Most of the earliest pieces bear the Federal trademark (a capital F within a shield). In 1931, the company issued its first mold-etched pattern, called "Georgian." In 1934, Federal manufactured its first chipped-mold design, "Mayfair." During the late '30s, the company used the paste-mold method to manufacture two other patterns, "Heritage" and "Columbia."

Hazel Atlas

The Hazel Atlas Glass Company of Clarksville, West Virginia, produced many popular machine-made, mold-etched patterns during the '30s, including a pressed pattern called "Moderntone" and a mold-etched pattern called "Cloverleaf." The company was primarily known for its household glassware. In fact, in a trade journal published in 1928, the company was dubbed the "world's largest tumbler factory." The company also made some of the ever popular Shirley Temple blue glass.

Indiana

The Indiana Glass Company of Dunkirk, Indiana, began making pressed patterns as well and hand-molded "Sandwich" glass in 1929. Later the company manufactured heavy, serviceable glass which was often used in soda fountains. Most of these early patterns were not named, but were sold by number. During the late '20s, the company made three mold-etched patterns: "Lorain," "Vernon," and "Number 612." These were the only mold-etched patterns manufactured by Indiana Glass.

Jeannette

The Jeannette Glass Company of Jeannette, Pennsylvania, made their first pressed pattern "Cubist" in pink. Pink and green were the first two colors used by the company. Jeannette made many successful mold-etched patterns including "Floral" and "Cherry Blossom." Jeannette Glass also made children's sets and is the only company to make cone-shaped pitchers.

Macbeth-Evans

In general, the Macbeth-Evans Glass Company of Charleroi, Pennsylvania, made the most delicate Depression glass. The company introduced its first mold-etched pattern in 1930 and during the late '30s developed two special patterns of glass called Monax and Cremax to compete with the china and pottery industry. In 1937, the company was purchased by Corning Glass Works of Corning, New York.

Other large manufacturers of depression glass include: Cambridge Glass Company of Cambridge, Ohio, the Imperial Glass Company of Bellaire, Ohio, United States Glass Company of Pittsburgh, Pennsylvania, and the Westmoreland Glass Company of Grapeville, Pennsylvania.

Most depression glass, like this pitcher, was made in transparent hues of amber, blue, yellow, pink and green.

Cheery yellow depression glass still brings sunshine to dinner tables.

Decorating magazines of the 30s suggested that the housewife coordinate her dinner dress with the color of her glassware.

Any piece of ebony Depression glass is highly desirable.

A decorous ebony sugar and creamer.

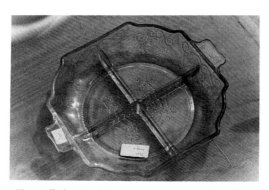

"Lorain", 4-part relish, manufactured by Indiana Glass, 1929-1932, valued at $3.00.

Repairing Depression Glass

Repairing glass is a difficult task and it is virtually impossible to camouflage the repair, and repairs do diminish the value of a piece. Two pieces can never be glued invisibly, even with transparent adhesive. Chips, cracks or missing pieces can be replaced by using casting resin, a clear liquid plastic which dries to a hard glass-like finish. Prepare the resin according to the manufacturer's directions. You may add coloring agents if you wish. Make a mold with masking tape around the chipped rim and fill the mold with resin. When the resin is dry, remove the mold, sand the repaired area and apply a thin coat of resin to it. Resin can also be used as a glue to mend broken pieces or strengthen cracks. Minor rim chips can be ground off.

Depression glassware was made for everyday use and will stand up to ordinary use today. You can use Depression glass to set your table and give it a bright nostalgic look. Depression glass can be put in a dishwasher; household detergents, unknown in the '30s, will not harm the glass.

Depression glass does crack easily. The glass was made quickly and cheaply and the flaws cause the pieces to crack when, for example, extremely hot food is placed in them. But most of the severely flawed pieces were broken long ago and are not on the collectors' market.

Cleaning Glassware

If the glassware is very dirty, soak it in a solution of ammoniated cleaner and water. That will loosen the dirt collected between the embossments of the pattern, and a toothbrush will help you remove the last particles. But before you soak any Depression glass, check to see if the piece has been repaired. The glue made prior to World War II is not waterproof and will disintegrate if you soak the piece too long. It is best to use repaired pieces only for display.

Many Depression glass pieces were made with chrome parts. Clean each part separately. You can polish the chrome but do not use an abrasive cleaner as '30s chrome was lightly plated and may wear through.

Many more plainly patterned plates show scratches from knives and forks. If you are going to use the plate, there is nothing you can do to hide the scratches. But if you choose to display your piece, the appearance can be somewhat improved by rubbing the surface with an almond stick or a light oil like baby oil.

Displaying Your Collection

Depression glass is an intricate part of our heritage and many people collect it simply as a memento of times gone by. But most of it can still be used. Depression glass will give your table a cheery look reminiscent of another era. You can really have fun if you combine it with Carnival glass or art glass. If you use crystal plates, you might want to use a colored or patterned ceramic plate underneath.

People are rediscovering the beauty of colored glass and recognizing it as a versatile decorative accessory. Colored glass can be used to complete the color scheme in any room of the house. Colored cookie jars can be filled with marbles or seashells and used to accent your decorating scheme. Kitchenware such as reamers, measuring cups and mixing bowls can be displayed on a shelf in the kitchen, easily accessible for use.

Depression glass looks great when displayed on a shelf with natural or artificial backlighting to show off the color and pattern. You can build shelves across a window or place your collection in a shadow box. Many collectors enclose their glassware in a well-lit, glass-fronted cabinet. (Enclosing your collection in a cabinet also has the added advantage of keeping the pieces free of dust.)

You can make an attractive display by grouping the glass according to color, pattern or type. Look at your friends' displays and use them as a source of inspiration. Or look for ideas in home decorating magazines or books devoted to collectibles. You may want to expand your collection by collecting related items such as advertisements from magazines, newspapers or almanacs or by collecting other similar promotional items.

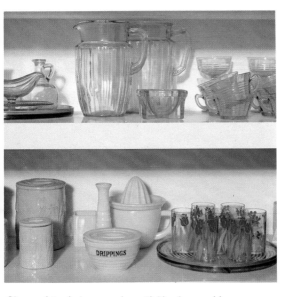

Clean, white shelves are a beautiful background for brilliantly-colored depression glass.

Measuring cups were popular promotional pieces, often used by refrigerator manufacturers.

Pretty green sherbets sold for less than a nickel; now they're worth $2.25.

Depression glass makes a dramatic display when highlighted by natural light.

"Lace Edge" 3-part relish dish, made by Hocking between 1935-1938.

The many surfaces of this glass catches light and creates an effect similar to that of expensive cut glass.

"Tea Room", Indiana Glass Co., 1926-1931, today valued at $75.00.

Complete sugar and creamer sets are rare.

Funky candleholder, popular during the Depression.

Cool cobalt blue is as popular today as it was during the Depression.

61

A
Guide to
Trademarks

Trademarks were either impressed into the glass or printed on paper labels which were glued onto the glass or packing case (it is rare to find a paper label these days). The impressed trademark is usually found directly in the center of the underside of the piece, although some trademarks were embossed on stems, sides, handles or other, less conspicuous spots.

AKRO AGATE COMPANY. "A-kro" with marbles in its beak and claws. Paper label or impressed into underside of glass. Akro Agate famous for glass marbles produced between 1914 and 1954. Trademark not always used but on pieces without trademark, Akro colors and marbelized effects unmistakable.

ANCHOR GLASS COMPANY. Paper label. Commercial glassware, jars, tableware.

ANCHOR HOCKING GLASS COMPANY. Paper label on all glassware.

BARTLETT-COLLINS GLASS COMPANY. Paper label. Handmade glassware until 1941, when company began using machines. Tableware and lamps.

CAMBRIDGE GLASS COMPANY. Tableware and occasional pieces.

CORNING GLASS WORKS. Paper label or etched into glass. First used by Macbeth-Evans Glass Company, bought by Corning in 1937.

DUNBAR GLASS CORPORATION. Paper label. Many fancy patterns of tableware and beverage sets.

DUNCAN AND MILLER GLASS COMPANY. Paper label. Best known for color reproductions of Early American pressed glass patterns.

FEDERAL GLASS COMPANY. Impressed on dinnerware, also paper label. Major manufacturer of machine-made, mold-etched dinnerware.

HAZEL-ATLAS GLASS COMPANY. Paper label and impressed on tableware. Once referred to as "world's largest tumbler factory."

HELLER COMPANY. Paper label. General glassware. This trademark used on items not made by Heller but with Heller-made metal attachments.

HOCKING GLASS COMPANY. Paper label used prior to merger with Anchor Glass Company (1938). One of leading manufacturers of machine-made, mold-etched glassware.

IMPERIAL GLASS COMPANY. Impressed on tableware. Not used after 1932. Known for imitation cut glass (called "Nu-Cut") and special color effects. Used oval trademark after becoming corporation in 1932.

INDIANA GLASS COMPANY. Paper label. Primarily tableware and tumblers.

JEANNETTE GLASS COMPANY. Impressed on glassware. Forerunner of automated glassmaking. Primarily tableware and kitchenware.

D. C. JENKINS GLASS COMPANY. Impressed on glass. Heavy glass often used in hotels and soda fountains.

MACBETH-EVANS GLASS COMPANY. See Corning Glass Works.

MARYLAND GLASS CORPORATION. Impressed on glass.

MCKEE GLASS COMPANY. Impressed on glass. Some paper labels. Handmade but moderately priced glassware of all kinds. Factories became automated during early 1940s.

MORGANTOWN GLASS WORKS. General glassware for home including tableware.

NEW MARTINSVILLE GLASS MANUFACTURING COMPANY. Utilitarian and decorative glassware. Also oval-shaped paper label.

L. E. SMITH. Impressed on glass between 1920 to 1935. Tableware, cookware, novelties.

UNITED STATES GLASS COMPANY. Embossed on glassware. U.S. Glass formed by merger of 18 glass factories in 1891. Of the 18, four important factories: Tiffin, expensive, handmade glass; Gas City and Glassport, machine-made kitchenware and tableware; and Pittsburgh, hand-decorated glassware.

WESTMORELAND GLASS COMPANY. Paper label used on almost all glassware.

This geometrically patterned vase is reminiscent of Fred Astaire and Busby Berkeley musicals.

Attractive swirled pattern was adapted from the decorative art styles popular during the 1930s.

Depression glass can even add a touch of class . . .

Custard cups used to serve the new "precooked" desserts of the 1930s.

Price Guide

The collector should remember that prices vary in different parts of the country. Wholesale prices are usually 40 – 50% percent lower than the prices listed in our guide.

ANCHOR HOCKING COMPANY

BLOCK OPTIC	GREEN	PINK	YELLOW	CRYSTAL
Berry bowl, 4¼"	3.00	3.00	— —	— —
Butter, covered	24.00	— —	— —	— —
Cereal bowl, 5¼"	3.75	3.75	— —	— —
Creamer, cone shape	— —	5.00	— —	— —
Cup and saucer	5.00	3.75	7.25	4.25
Dish, candy, covered	17.00	— —	25.00	— —
Goblet, 5"	— —	— —	10.00	4.75 – 8.25
Plate, 6"	1.50	1.75	2.00	1.50

Plate, 10¼"	6.00	6.75 – 10.00	—	5.75
Sherbet, footed	7.00	6.50	10.00	5.00
Sugar and creamer, cone shape	10.00	7.00	—	—
Tumbler, footed, 9 oz.	—	—	—	8.25

BUBBLE	PINK	GREEN	CRYSTAL
Berry bowl, 8⅜"	2.50 – 8.00	2.50	1.75
Bowl, 5¼"	—	3.00 – 5.50	1.50
Candlesticks, pair	—	—	9.50
Creamer	—	3.25 – 10.00	4.25
Cup and saucer	—	4.50 – 4.75	1.00
Goblet, 4½"	—	3.75	—
Plate, 6¾"	—	1.75 – 3.25	1.00
Platter, oval, 12"	—	—	3.00
Sugar and creamer	—	5.50 – 12.00	6.50 – 10.50
Tumbler, flat, 12 oz.	—	—	10.00

CAMEO	PINK	GREEN	YELLOW	CRYSTAL
Berry bowl, 4½"	—	3.25	—	—
Bowl, vegetable, 9"	—	6.75	—	—
Butter, covered	—	75.00–125.00	—	—
Compote	—	13.00–15.50	—	—
Cup and saucer	—	6.25–10.00	5.00–10.00	3.25
Dish, candy, 4"	—	20.50–34.00	—	—
Goblet, 4"	—	33.00–40.00	—	—
Pitcher, rope trim, 8½"	—	33.50	—	—
Plate, 6"	—	1.50–3.50	—	2.00–10.00
Plate, 10"	16.00	6.00–7.00	4.75	—
Plate, grill, 10½"	—	3.75–6.00	—	—
Salt and pepper, footed	—	24.00–50.00	—	—
Sugar and creamer, 4¼"	82.00	25.00	—	—
Syrup, 5¾"	—	85.00–122.00	—	—
Tumbler, footed, 5"	—	10.00–20.00	8.00–13.00	6.25–7.25

COLONIAL	GREEN	PINK	CRYSTAL	OPAQUE CREAM
Berry bowl, 4½"	6.00	— —	— —	— —
Bowl, flat soup, 7"	— —	— —	8.75	— —
Creamer, 5"	4.25 – 9.75	9.75	— —	— —
Cup and saucer	36.00 – 46.00	— —	— —	11.00
Goblet, 4"	18.25	— —	3.50 – 4.75	— —
Pitcher, ice lip, 54 oz.	22.75	22.00 – 25.00	— —	— —
Plate, 6"	1.75 – 4.25	2.00 – 2.75	1.25 – 1.75	— —
Plate, 10"	12.75 – 22.25	4.25 – 7.00	7.25 – 9.25	— —
Salt and pepper	46.00 – 81.00	40.00 – 90.00	36.00	— —
Sugar. covered, 5"	12.25 – 15.25	4.25 – 26.00	6.75 – 12.25	— —
Tumbler, footed, 3¼"	— —	5.25	2.75	— —

CORONATION	PINK	RED	CRYSTAL
Berry bowl, 4¼"	— —	1.75 – 3.25	— —
Berry set, 5 piece	— —	15.00 – 17.00	— —
Bowl, 2 handles, 8"	6.75	5.25 – 7.25	— —
Cup and saucer	3.75 – 4.25	— —	— —
Plate, 6"	1.25 – 3.25	— —	2.00
Plate, 9½"	1.75	— —	— —
Tumbler, footed, 5"	5.25 – 6.25	— —	5.25

FORTUNE	PINK	CRYSTAL
Berry bowl, 4"	1.50 – 2.75	1.00
Dish, candy, covered	4.25 – 9.25	5.25 – 6.25
Plate, 6"	1.50	— —
Saucer	2.00 – 2.75	— —
Tumbler, 4"	3.75	— —

HOBNAIL	PINK	CRYSTAL
Bowl, ruffled, 10"	39.00	—
Creamer, footed	—	4.75
Cup	2.25 – 4.25	1.75 – 2.75
Decanter, stopper, 32 oz.	—	13.00
Goblet, 8 oz.	—	1.50
Pitcher, 18 oz.	—	8.00 – 11.25
Plate, 6"	1.25 – 2.25	1.00
Sherbet	2.25 – 3.00	—
Tumbler, footed, 3¼"	—	3.25
Vase, footed, 6½"	29.00	—

LACE EDGE	PINK	CRYSTAL
Bowl, 6⅜"	4.75 – 7.75	2.75 – 6.75
Bowl, 9½"	4.50 – 12.50	7.00
Butter, covered	31.00 – 46.00	33.00
Cookie jar, covered	– –	26.00
Cup and saucer	12.75 – 15.00	– –
Plate, 10½"	8.25 – 11.25	9.25 – 10.25
Plate, grill, 10½"	7.75	7.25
Relish, 3 part, 7½"	24.00	11.00
Server, center handle	56.00	– –
Sugar	7.00 – 7.75	9.00
Tumbler, footed, 5"	6.00 – 24.50	18.50

MANHATTAN	PINK	GREEN	CRYSTAL
Ashtray, 4"	—	—	4.00 – 5.00
Berry bowl, 2 handles	3.25	—	3.75
Candleholders, square, 4½", pair	—	—	6.75
Candy container, covered	10.00	—	10.50
Compote, 5¾"	3.00 – 6.75	—	1.75 – 9.75
Creamer, oval	2.50 – 4.25	—	2.25 – 3.25
Cup and saucer	8.25	—	4.25
Pitcher, 42 oz.	13.50 – 22.50	—	4.25 – 9.25
Plate, 8½"	—	—	2.75 – 5.25
Salt and pepper, 2"	12.50 – 20.50	—	8.50 – 15.50
Sherbet, flat, 2¼"	3.25	—	4.75
Sugar and creamer, oval	4.50 – 18.50	—	4.75 – 10.00
Tumbler, footed	4.00 – 6.25	5.25	—
Water set, 7 piece	—	—	34.00

MAYFAIR	PINK	GREEN	YELLOW	BLUE
Bowl, 5½"	5.25 – 8.75	—	97.00	—
Butter, covered	28.00 – 36.00	—	—	—
Candy Dish, covered	—	410.00 – 510.00	360.00	87.00
Celery, divided, 10"	16.00	—	—	21.00
Cookie jar, covered	17.00 – 21.50	410.00	—	—
Cup and saucer	8.25 – 15.75	—	—	28.00 – 33.00
Goblet, 7¼"	52.00	—	—	52.00 – 57.00
Pitcher, 6", 37 oz.	15.50 – 18.50	—	—	42.00 – 57.00
Plate, 8½"	6.75 – 9.75	—	62.00	14.00 – 15.00
Salt and pepper, flat	27.00 – 33.00	—	525.00	105.00 – 140.00
Soup, cream, 5"	11.75 – 15.25	—	—	—
Tumbler, 3½"	19.00	—	—	43.00
Whiskey, 2¼"	50.00	—	—	—

MISS AMERICA	PINK	GREEN	CRYSTAL
Berry bowl, 6¼"	4.25– 8.75	––	3.25
Bowl, oval, 10"	7.75– 12.25	––	5.75– 11.75
Butter, covered	130.00	––	135.00
Candy container, covered, 11½"	72.00	––	40.00
Celery, 10½"	8.25– 10.25	––	4.25– 5.25
Coaster, 5¾"	13.75– 17.75	––	5.25– 9.25
Compote, 5"	7.00– 10.75	––	5.25– 10.25
Creamer	7.00– 10.00	––	3.75– 6.25
Cup	7.00– 11.75	8.25– 9.25	2.75– 6.25
Goblet, 4¾"	36.00	––	16.00
Pitcher, ice lip, 8½"	72.00	––	57.00
Plate, 8½"	6.25– 9.25	2.25– 4.25
Relish, 4 section, 8¾"	8.75	5.25	––
Salt and pepper	31.00	––	13.25– 20.25
Sugar and creamer	14.25– 22.25	––	8.25– 10.25
Tumbler, footed, 5 oz.	23.50– 38.00	––	15.25

OLD CAFE	PINK	CRYSTAL
Bowl, closed handles, 9"	3.50	3.75
Candy dish, closed handles, 8"	4.25	5.25
Cup and saucer	4.25 – 6.75	– –
Plate, 6"	2.25	1.50
Sherbet, footed	– –	2.75
Tumbler, 4"	2.75	– –
Vase, 7¼"	– –	6.25

PRINCESS	GREEN	PINK	YELLOW
Berry bowl, 4½"	13.50	4.50	—
Bowl, oval, 10"	7.00 – 9.75	8.75	17.50 – 25.50
Butter, covered	38.00 – 52.00	47.00 – 57.00	—
Candy container, covered	28.00	28.00	—
Creamer	6.00 – 8.00	5.25 – 7.75	5.25 – 7.75
Cup and saucer	6.25 – 8.75	4.75 – 6.75	5.00 – 7.75
Pitcher, 8"	21.00 – 28.00	23.00 – 25.00	36.00 – 43.00
Plate, 8"	4.25 – 7.75	3.75 – 4.25	3.25 – 5.25
Plate, grill, 9"	6.75	—	—
Relish, 4 section	13.50	7.50 – 10.50	—
Salt and pepper	23.00 – 31.00	23.50 – 29.00	46.00 – 66.00
Sugar, open	6.50	5.50	—
Tumbler, flat, 9 oz.	14.50	11.00	—
Water set, 9 piece	—	165.00	—

QUEEN MARY	PINK	RED	CRYSTAL
Ashtray	— —	2.75 – 3.75	2.75
Bowl, handle, 4"	1.75	— —	2.25
Bowl, 5"	2.75	— —	1.25 – 2.75
Butter, covered	32.00 – 70.00	— —	15.50 – 18.50
Candy dish, covered	10.50 – 13.50	— —	13.50 – 19.00
Coaster	2.25	— —	1.75
Creamer	2.75	— —	3.00
Cup and saucer	4.00	— —	5.00
Plate, 6"	1.25	— —	1.25
Relish, 3 section, 12"	— —	— —	5.25
Sherbet	1.75 – 4.25	— —	— —
Sugar and creamer	4.25 – 8.25	— —	4.25 – 7.25
Tumbler, footed, 10 oz.	— —	— —	11.25

RING	GREEN	BLUE	CRYSTAL
Bowl, 8"	3.75	— —	— —
Cocktail shaker, aluminum top	— —	— —	9.50
Cup, platinum rings	2.00	— —	2.00
Decanter set	— —	21.00	— —
Goblet, 7½"	5.25	— —	4.75 – 6.25
Plate, off-center ring, 6"	2.00	— —	4.75
Salt and pepper	— —	— —	8.25
Server, center handle	15.25 – 16.75	— —	4.25 – 8.25
Sherbet, 4¾"	4.25	— —	2.50
Tumbler, flat, 3½"	3.25	— —	3.50
Whiskey set, 6 piece	— —	— —	23.00

ROULETTE	GREEN	PINK
Bowl, 9"	5.25 – 9.75	— —
Cup and saucer	2.50 – 5.75	4.25
Plate, 6"	1.50	— —
Pitcher, 8"	— —	17.00
Tumbler, 9 oz.	5.25	5.25
Whiskey, 2½"	5.75	— —

SANDWICH	PINK	CRYSTAL
Bowl, scalloped, 8"	12.50	— —
Bowl, smooth, 8"	10.50	— —
Butter, covered	— —	23.00
Cookie jar, covered	— —	16.00
Creamer	— —	3.75

		GREEN
Cup and saucer	— —	2.75 – 4.75
Pitcher, ice lip, 2 qt.	— —	42.00
Plate, 9"	— —	3.00 – 5.25
Sugar and creamer, covered	— —	13.00
Tumbler, 9 oz.	— —	5.50

SPIRAL	GREEN
Bowl, 8"	5.25
Butter, covered	10.50
Champagne	4.25
Creamer, footed	4.25 – 5.25
Cup and saucer	3.25
Pitcher, rope rim, 7⅝"	19.00

FEDERAL GLASS COMPANY

COLONIAL FLUTED	GREEN
Berry bowl, 4″	2.50
Creamer	2.75 – 5.25
Cup and saucer	3.50
Plate, 6″	1.50
Sherbet	2.25
Sugar and creamer	7.00 – 10.25

COLUMBIA	PINK	CRYSTAL
Bowl, 5″	— —	1.75 – 6.00
Butter, covered	— —	7.75 – 26.00
Cordial, 1 oz.	— —	6.25

	PINK	AMBER	CRYSTAL
Cup and saucer		—	2.00 – 5.50
Plate, 6"		4.00	1.00 – 3.75
Plate, 9½"		7.25	2.25 – 5.75
Plate, chop, 11¾"		—	3.75 – 5.25

DIANA	PINK	AMBER	CRYSTAL
Bowl, 5"	1.75 – 3.25	3.75	2.75 – 3.75
Candy dish, covered	13.00 – 22.00	9.50 – 18.00	8.00
Creamer	—	4.75	2.25
Cup and saucer	8.25	5.25 – 6.25	3.25 – 4.25
Plate, 6"	2.00	1.00 – 2.00	1.00 – 3.25
Plate, 9½"	2.25 – 5.25	2.25 – 5.25	3.00
Salt and pepper	11.50 – 28.00	21.00 – 70.00	11.50
Soup, cream, 5½"	2.25	6.25 – 8.75	2.50 – 4.25
Sherbet	3.50	—	—
Sugar and creamer	6.25	—	—

FEDERAL GLASS COMPANY

GEORGIAN	GREEN	PINK	CRYSTAL
Berry bowl, 4½"	2.50 – 5.25	—	3.75
Butter, covered	36.00 – 67.00	—	43.00
Cake server, center handle	19.00	—	—
Creamer, footed, 3"	4.25 – 6.25	—	5.75
Cup and saucer	5.75 – 8.25	—	6.25 – 7.75
Plate, 6"	1.75 – 3.75	—	2.25
Platter, 11½"	36.00	—	27.00
Sherbet	2.25 – 6.50	—	4.75 – 6.00
Sugar, open	—	6.00	—
Tumbler, 4"	4.00 – 25.00	—	2.75

HERITAGE	GREEN	CRYSTAL
Berry bowl, 5"	25.00	2.00 – 4.00
Creamer	– –	5.50 – 7.50
Cup and saucer	– –	2.50 – 5.50
Plate, 6"	– –	1.25
Sugar and creamer, open	– –	12.50 – 20.00

HONEYCOMB	PINK	GREEN
Cup	– –	2.25
Ice bucket	8.25	– –
Pitcher, 5"	– –	6.75
Plate, 6"	– –	1.00
Sugar and creamer	5.25	– –
Tumbler, 5¾"	6.25	5.25

MADRID	PINK	GREEN	BLUE	AMBER	CRYSTAL
Berry bowl, 5"	3.25	4.25	—	1.75 – 4.00	—
Butter, covered	—	52.00 – 75.00	—	37.00 – 62.00	97.00
Candlesticks, 2¼", pair	15.50	—	—	15.50	12.50
Cookie Jar, covered	22.00 – 25.00	—	—	19.00 – 25.00	17.00 – 31.00
Creamer	—	3.50 – 6.75	11.25	2.75	4.25
Cup and saucer	—	5.75 – 7.25	—	3.75 – 6.25	—
Hot plate and coaster	—	30.00	—	20.00 – 37.00	20.00
Jar, jam, 7"	—	—	14.50	6.25 – 9.75	2.25 – 4.25
Pitcher, square, 60 oz.	—	92.00	—	29.00	40.00
Plate, 6"	—	—	5.25	1.75 – 4.75	1.25 – 2.75
Platter, oval, 11½"	—	7.50	10.50	9.50	9.50
Salt and pepper, footed	—	70.00	—	36.00	45.00
Sugar and creamer, open	—	—	21.00	6.00 – 10.50	—
Tumbler, flat, 5½"	—	—	—	13.00	19.00

MAYFAIR	AMBER	GREEN	CRYSTAL
Bowl, 2 handles, 10"	-- --	-- --	9.50
Bowl, scalloped, 12"	-- --	16.50	-- --
Cup	-- --	-- --	5.25
Plate, 6¾"	3.25	-- --	4.25
Plate, grill, 9½"	1.50 – 6.75	-- --	3.75
Saucer	2.25 – 3.75	-- --	-- --
Sugar, footed	4.75 – 8.25	-- --	-- --

NORMANDIE	PINK	AMBER	GREEN	CRYSTAL	IRIDESCENT ORANGE
Berry bowl, 5"	3.25 – 5.25	2.75 – 3.75	— —	— —	1.75 – 5.50
Bowl, 8½"	16.00	6.25 – 14.00	— —	— —	5.25 – 8.25
Bowl, oval, 10"	— —	7.25 – 10.25	— —	— —	9.25
Creamer, footed	— —	4.75 – 5.75	— —	— —	2.75 – 4.25
Cup and saucer	4.25 – 6.75	3.25 – 6.00	— —	4.75	4.25 – 6.75
Pitcher, 8"	— —	27.00 – 45.00	— —	— —	— —
Plate, 6"	1.75 – 3.25	1.00 – 2.25	— —	— —	2.00
Plate, 9¼"	3.75	2.75 – 5.25	6.25	— —	7.25 – 8.25
Plate, grill, 11"	4.25	3.75 – 8.00	— —	— —	2.75 – 5.25
Salt and pepper	25.00 – 35.00	26.00 – 34.00	— —	— —	— —
Sherbet, footed	2.25 – 5.25	2.25 – 6.75	— —	— —	3.25 – 6.00
Sugar, open	— —	3.50 – 5.75	— —	— —	3.25

PATRICIAN	PINK	GREEN	AMBER	CRYSTAL
Berry bowl, 8½"	8.25 – 13.00	8.25 – 9.75	5.75 – 12.00	8.25
Bowl, oval, 12"	7.75	11.50	9.25 – 15.00	— —
Butter, covered	180.00	75.00	32.00 – 52.00	60.00
Cookie jar, covered	— —	16.00 – 175.00	26.00 – 38.00	36.00
Cup and saucer	9.00	6.00 – 9.25	7.00 – 9.75	— —
Pitcher, 8"	87.00	— —	40.00 – 50.00	— —
Plate, 9"	3.25 – 4.75	4.00 – 6.25	3.25 – 5.25	3.25
Plate, grill, 10½"	7.75	7.25	6.25	5.25
Platter, oval, 11½"	9.25	— —	14.50	5.25
Salt and pepper	56.00 – 87.00	29.00 – 40.00	18.50 – 28.00	26.00
Sherbet	5.00	3.25 – 6.75	3.75 – 6.25	— —
Sugar and creamer, covered	— —	46.00	25.00	— —
Tumbler, flat, 5 oz.	— —	— —	11.00	— —
Tumbler, footed, 5¼"	— —	17.00	— —	— —

FEDERAL GLASS COMPANY

SHARON	PINK	GREEN	AMBER	CRYSTAL
Berry bowl, 5″	4.50	6.00	4.00	— —
Bowl, oval, 9½″	8.00 – 14.00	11.00	7.00	— —
Butter, covered	26.00 – 36.00	60.00	40.00	— —
Cake plate, footed, 11½″	16.00	30.00	— —	— —
Cake plate, metal lid	— —	— —	— —	16.00
Candy dish, covered	22.00 – 32.00	97.00	20.00 – 24.00	— —
Cup and saucer	7.00	8.75 – 11.00	2.00 – 5.75	— —
Jar, jam, 7½″	42.00	18.00 – 25.00	12.50 – 20.00	— —
Plate, 6″	2.00 – 6.00	3.25	2.25 – 3.25	— —
Plate, 9½″	6.00 – 11.00	8.00	4.25 – 5.75	— —
Salt and pepper	30.00	42.00 – 62.00	20.00 – 25.00	— —
Soup, cream, 5″	13.00 – 17.00	16.00	9.25 – 15.50	— —
Sugar and creamer, covered	18.00 – 23.00	— —	21.00	— —
Tumbler, 9 oz.	15.00	29.00	— —	— —

SYLVAN	AMBER	GREEN	CRYSTAL
Berry bowl, 5"	—	—	7.75 – 10.00
Bowl, oval, 10"	—	16.00 – 21.00	—
Butter, covered	—	200.00 – 225.00	—
Creamer	—	16.00 – 19.00	—
Cup and saucer	—	15.00 – 21.00	—
Pitcher, 8½"	—	460.00 – 500.00	—
Plate, 5¾"	4.25	5.50 – 10.50	—
Plate, grill, 10½"	—	12.50	7.75
Platter, oval, 11¼"	37.00	21.00	—
Sherbet, cone shape, footed	9.25	10.50	—
Tumbler, flat, 5½"	—	77.00	—

HAZEL ATLAS GLASS COMPANY

CLOVERLEAF	GREEN	PINK	YELLOW	CRYSTAL	BLACK
Ashtray, 5¾"	— —	— —	— —	— —	57.00
Bowl, 4"	6.00 – 9.00	6.25 – 7.75	— —	— —	— —
Creamer	— —	— —	9.75	6.25	6.75 – 12.25
Cup and saucer	4.00 – 6.75	3.75 – 6.75	15.50	3.25 – 4.25	6.00 – 13.00
Plate, 6"	1.50 – 3.00	— —	3.00	— —	12.75 – 20.00
Plate, 8"	3.25 – 11.25	2.25 – 4.25	5.00	— —	4.75 – 9.50
Salt and pepper	15.00 – 26.00	— —	— —	— —	35.00 – 60.00
Sherbet, footed, 3"	3.75 – 4.75	2.75 – 6.25	5.25 – 8.25	1.50	6.25 – 14.50
Sugar	4.75	— —	8.25	— —	6.25 – 9.75
Tumbler, flat, 4"	15.00	14.50	— —	— —	— —

FLORENTINE	PINK	AMBER	GREEN	BLUE	YELLOW	CRYSTAL
Ashtray, 5½"	— —	— —	13.75 – 20.00	— —	20.00	— —
Bowl, 4½"	6.25	— —	— —	— —	— —	2.50
Candlesticks, 2¾", pair	— —	— —	— —	— —	31.00	26.00
Coaster	8.25	— —	7.75	— —	9.25 – 12.50	— —
Creamer	— —	— —	7.75	— —	6.00 – 7.00	3.25
Cup and saucer	— —	— —	3.75 – 10.50	— —	7.50	2.75 – 5.50
Custard	— —	— —	6.75	— —	— —	9.25
Pitcher, cone shape, 7½"	— —	— —	— —	— —	21.00	19.00
Plate, 6"	2.75	— —	2.25 – 5.25	— —	2.25 – 3.75	1.50
Plate, 10"	— —	— —	4.75 – 7.25	— —	3.25 – 7.75	2.75 – 3.75
Plate, grill, 10"	— —	4.25	— —	— —	— —	— —
Salt shaker	— —	— —	8.25	— —	14.50	10.50
Sherbet	— —	— —	— —	— —	4.25 – 8.25	2.75
Soup, cream	— —	— —	— —	26.00	— —	2.75
Sugar	3.75	— —	3.25 – 5.25	— —	4.25 – 5.75	3.25 – 4.75
Tumbler, flat, 4"	6.25 – 8.25	— —	8.00	— —	8.25 – 10.75	3.25 – 8.00

MODERNTONE	BLUE	PURPLE	WHITE	CRYSTAL
Bowl, 8¾"	14.50 – 20.50	—	—	12.75
Butter, metal cover	52.00 – 62.00	—	—	—
Creamer	2.75 – 5.25	3.25 – 5.25	2.25	1.75
Cup and saucer	4.00 – 5.50	4.50	—	—
Plate, 7¾"	3.25 – 5.25	2.50	—	—
Plate, 8⅞"	3.25 – 7.25	3.25 – 4.75	—	1.75
Platter, oval, 12"	8.25 – 12.75	8.25	—	10.75 – 12.75
Salt and pepper	13.25 – 18.75	13.00	4.75 – 12.25	—
Soup, cream, 4¾"	4.25 – 8.25	—	1.75	3.25
Sugar, open	3.00 – 5.25	3.25 – 5.25	—	—
Tumbler, 9 oz.	6.25 – 12.25	—	—	—

OLD FLORENTINE	PINK	BLUE	GREEN	YELLOW	CRYSTAL
Berry bowl, 8½"	—	—	12.75	16.25	—
Bowl, 5"	7.00	10.50	—	—	—
Butter, covered	130.00	—	57.00 – 87.00	155.00	—
Creamer	4.75 – 6.75	—	4.75 – 6.75	7.00	2.50 – 4.25
Cup and saucer	5.75 – 7.25	—	7.00	—	3.75 – 5.75
Pitcher, footed, 6½"	34.00	—	28.00	—	21.00
Plate, 8½"	2.75 – 4.25	—	4.00 – 5.25	—	1.50 – 3.75
Plate, grill, 10"	—	—	4.00 – 5.75	7.50	—
Platter, oval, 11½"	—	—	10.00	—	—
Salt and pepper	28.00 – 38.00	—	18.00 – 21.00	—	15.50 – 20.50
Sherbet	3.00 – 6.25	31.00 – 35.00	2.75 – 4.75	5.75 – 9.75	—
Sugar	4.75	—	5.00	—	3.75
Tumbler, 4¾"	12.75	—	10.25	—	6.25

RIBBON	GREEN	CRYSTAL
Berry bowl, 4"	4.75	— —
Bowl, 8"	— —	7.25
Creamer	3.00	4.25
Cup and saucer	6.75	4.25
Plate, 6¼"	2.00	1.25
Plate, 8"	1.75 – 3.25	3.25
Salt and pepper	9.50 – 13.50	17.00
Sherbet	3.00	3.50
Sugar	3.00 – 4.00	3.75
Tumbler, footed, 13 oz.	7.00	— —

ROYAL LACE	PINK	GREEN	PURPLE	BLUE	CRYSTAL
Berry bowl, 10"	7.75 – 9.25	21.00	— —	23.00	— —
Bowl, 3 legs, ruffled edge, 10"	— —	31.00	— —	— —	15.50

Cup and saucer	8.00	9.75 – 12.50	— —	15.00 – 19.50	7.75
Pitcher, 68 oz.	33.00 – 40.00	76.00	— —	66.00	26.00
Plate, 8½"	86.00	6.25 – 8.25	— —	8.75 – 16.50	6.75
Platter, oval, 13"	10.50	15.50 – 24.00	— —	23.00 – 27.00	12.50
Sherbet, metal holder	— —	— —	26.00	10.50 – 15.00	— —
Soup, cream, 4¾"	— —	6.25 – 8.25	— —	12.75 – 18.25	3.75 – 6.25
Sugar, open	— —	6.25 – 7.75	— —	14.75	3.25 – 5.75
Tumbler, 3½"	8.75 – 10.25	— —	— —	16.50 – 18.50	5.25 – 8.25

STARLIGHT	WHITE	CRYSTAL
Bowl, 11½"	— —	9.25
Creamer, oval	— —	3.25
Cup and saucer	— —	2.75
Plate, 8½"	— —	2.25 – 3.75
Plate, 9"	3.75	— —
Salt and pepper	— —	10.25 – 12.75
Sugar, oval	— —	3.25

INDIANA GLASS COMPANY

NO. 612	GREEN	YELLOW
Bowl, 8½"	12.75	— —
Bowl, oval, 10½"	14.75	13.00
Candy dish, covered, metal holder	155.00	— —
Creamer	5.25 – 9.75	7.25
Cup and saucer	5.25 – 10.00	7.50
Pitcher, 8½"	170.00	— —
Plate, 6"	1.50 – 2.75	2.00 – 6.00
Plate, 8⅜"	2.00 – 5.25	6.00
Platter, oval, 10¾"	12.25	13.50
Relish, footed, 3 section	7.25 – 15.50	16.50
Sugar, open	5.25 – 10.25	5.75

NO. 615

	GREEN	YELLOW	CRYSTAL
Bowl, 8"	30.00	80.00	——
Creamer, footed	5.25	10.00	——
Cup and saucer	15.50	6.25–12.25	5.25–12.25
Plate, 7¾"	4.25–7.25	5.25–7.25	2.25–3.75
Relish, handle, 4 section	——	7.25–15.00	10.50
Tumbler, footed, 4¾"	——	12.75	12.50

NO. 616

	YELLOW	GREEN	CRYSTAL
Creamer	——	——	6.25
Cup and saucer	——	12.75	6.75
Plate, 8"	6.50	6.25–8.75	4.25
Tumbler, footed, 5"	——	——	8.25
Vase, 7¾"	36.00	——	——

NO. 618	AMBER	CRYSTAL
Ashtray, 4½"	— —	7.25 – 10.25
Bowl, 6"	— —	6.75 – 12.75
Cup and saucer	6.25	4.75 – 7.50
Plate, 6"	2.50	1.75 – 3.75
Plate, 8⅜"	3.75 – 8.50	2.25 – 6.25
Soup, cream, 4⅝"	11.50 – 14.50	12.25
Sugar and creamer	8.25 – 10.50	— —
Tumbler, 4½", 12 oz.	— —	18.50

NO. 620	AMBER	CRYSTAL
Berry bowl, 4½"	2.75	— —
Bowl, 7⅜"	7.00	— —
Creamer, footed	2.25 – 4.25	— —

Cup and saucer	3.50 – 4.75	2.75 – 4.75
Plate, 8⅜"	1.75 – 4.00	2.25
Plate, 11½"	5.25 – 7.00	3.25 – 5.25
Relish, 3 section, 8⅜"	5.00	— —
Sherbet, footed	1.25 – 4.75	— —
Sugar, footed	3.25 – 4.50	3.75

TEA ROOM	PINK	GREEN
Bowl, oval, 9"	26.00	— —
Ice bucket	— —	23.00 – 26.00
Pitcher, 64 oz.	66.00	— —
Salt and pepper	21.00	— —
Sherbet	3.75 – 7.75	— —
Sugar and creamer, rectangular	17.00	18.50
Toothpick holder	— —	15.50
Tumbler, 9 oz.	9.25	— —

JEANNETTE GLASS COMPANY

ADAM	PINK	GREEN
Ashtray, 4½"	7.00 – 20.00	10.50 – 15.50
Berry bowl, 4¾"	4.50 – 7.25	8.25
Bowl, covered, 9"	12.75 – 29.00	12.50 – 31.00
Butter, covered	53.00 – 230.00	170.00 – 275.00
Cake plate, footed, 10"	5.50 – 10.50	10.50
Candlesticks, 4", pair	28.00 – 36.00	39.00 – 66.00
Candy container, covered	29.00	26.00
Creamer	5.25 – 9.25	6.50
Cup and saucer	10.50 – 15.00	11.50 – 15.00
Plate, grill, 9"	4.75 – 9.75	5.50 – 9.75
Plate, square, 9"	5.75 – 10.50	6.25 – 11.25
Relish, divided, 8"	3.75 – 9.75	7.75
Sugar, covered	14.25 – 19.75	17.75

CHERRY BLOSSOM	PINK	GREEN	BLUE
Berry bowl, 4¾"	5.50 – 7.75	– –	– –
Bowl, oval, 9"	10.75 – 15.50	10.75 – 29.00	– –
Butter, covered	43.00 – 81.00	62.00 – 75.00	190.00
Child's set, 14 piece	142.00	– –	– –
Coaster	6.75 – 12.50	6.25 – 9.25	– –
Creamer	6.00 – 10.50	6.25 – 9.25	11.75 – 15.50
Cup and saucer	7.50 – 26.00	13.75 – 16.50	15.25
Mug, 7 oz.	130.00	127.00	– –
Plate, 9"	8.25 – 10.25	9.25 – 14.50	9.25 – 12.25
Platter, oval, 11"	13.50	– –	28.00
Sherbet	5.25 – 8.25	5.75 – 10.50	12.75 – 17.75
Sugar	5.25 – 7.00	6.25 – 8.25	11.25 – 15.50
Tray, handles, 10½"	14.50	14.50	13.50
Tumbler, flat, 4¼"	11.25	12.25	– –
Tumbler, scalloped foot, 4½"	18.50	23.00	21.00

JEANNETTE GLASS COMPANY

CUBIST	PINK	GREEN	CRYSTAL
Bowl, 6½"	2.75 – 5.75	— —	3.00
Butter, covered	28.00 – 43.00	18.75 – 43.00	— —
Candy container, covered	17.50	18.50	— —
Creamer, 2"	1.75 – 3.75	— —	1.00 – 2.00
Plate, 6"	1.00 – 2.00	2.00	1.00
Salt and pepper	7.50 – 12.50	11.00 – 21.00	— —
Sugar, 2"	2.00	— —	1.00 – 2.00

DORIC	PINK	GREEN	BLUE	CRYSTAL
Berry bowl, 4½"	1.50 – 3.75	— —	— —	— —
Butter, covered	36.00 – 60.00	46.00 – 66.00	— —	— —
Candy dish, 3 part	1.25 – 5.75	4.00	2.75 – 5.25	— —
Coaster	2.75 – 10.50	10.50	— —	— —

Creamer	—	6.50 – 8.00	—	22.00
Cup and saucer	4.75 – 6.75	5.25 – 7.75	—	—
Plate, 6"	2.00 – 3.50	2.00	—	—
Platter, oval, 12"	8.75	7.25 – 10.50	—	—
Sherbet	3.50	7.25	2.25 – 6.25	—
Sugar, covered	13.00	12.00 – 20.00	—	—
Tray, 8" × 8"	3.75 – 8.25	5.25	—	—

FLORAL	PINK	GREEN	CRYSTAL
Berry bowl, 4"	4.50 – 8.25	6.25	—
Bowl, oval, 9"	7.25 – 8.75	7.25 – 9.50	—
Butter, covered	49.00 – 92.00	46.00 – 62.00	—
Creamer	3.50 – 4.50	7.00 – 8.00	—
Cup and saucer	6.75 – 9.25	7.75 – 10.25	—
Pitcher, cone shape, footed, 7"	—	16.50	—
Plate, 6"	1.75 – 3.25	1.75 – 3.25	—
Platter, oval, 10¾"	7.25	8.25	—

HOMESPUN	PINK	CRYSTAL
Bowl, 4½"	5.25	— —
Butter, covered	35.00	61.00
Cup and saucer	4.00 – 6.75	— —
Plate, 6"	1.50 – 2.25	1.50
Plate, 9¼"	3.75 – 6.75	5.25
Tumbler, flat, 5¼"	— —	6.75

IRIS	PINK	CRYSTAL
Bowl, ruffled, 5"	— —	2.25 – 3.75
Bowl, straight edge, 5"	— —	2.50
Butter, covered	— —	15.25 – 19.25
Coaster	— —	23.00
Cup and saucer	— —	6.50 – 9.75

	PINK	GREEN
Goblet, 4"	—	5.75 – 8.25
Pitcher, 9½"	—	12.75 – 15.25
Plate, 8"	20.50	18.75
Sugar and creamer, open	—	6.50
Tumbler, footed, 7"	—	5.00 – 9.75

SIERRA	PINK	GREEN
Berry bowl, 8½"	7.50 – 8.75	7.50 – 10.00
Bowl, oval, 9¼"	10.00 – 14.50	22.50
Butter, covered	30.50 – 38.00	32.50 – 45.50
Creamer	5.75 – 8.75	7.25 – 8.75
Cup and saucer	4.25 – 8.75	7.75 – 9.50
Pitcher, 6½"	26.00 – 36.00	41.00
Plate, 9"	3.75 – 7.50	6.25 – 8.00
Salt and pepper	16.25 – 28.00	20.50 – 25.50
Sugar, open	5.25	7.75
Tumbler, footed, 4½"	15.25	18.75

SWIRL	PINK	BLUE	BLUE – GREEN
Bowl, 5¼"	1.50 – 4.25	6.25	5.00 – 8.25
Bowl, 9"	6.00	15.25	9.25 – 14.25
Candy dish, covered	58.00	—	51.00 – 70.00
Creamer, footed	3.50 – 4.25	—	4.25 – 6.25
Cup and saucer	5.25	—	5.75 – 7.75
Plate, 6½"	1.75	2.00	4.75
Salt and pepper	—	—	18.75 – 25.50
Sugar, footed	—	—	6.00
Tumbler, flat, 9 oz.	5.25	—	11.25

WINDSOR	PINK	GREEN	BLUE	CRYSTAL
Ashtray	16.50 – 25.50	26.00 – 36.00	31.00 – 40.00	— —
Berry bowl, 4¾"	3.50	— —	— —	3.00
Butter, covered	24.00 – 30.00	50.00 – 76.00	— —	15.25 – 25.50
Cup and saucer	5.00	6.25 – 7.75	— —	3.75
Pitcher, 16 oz.	25.50	— —	— —	8.25
Plate, 9"	3.25 – 6.25	— —	— —	3.00
Sherbet	2.25 – 5.75	3.75 – 4.75	— —	— —
Sugar and creamer, covered	15.00	— —	— —	10.00
Tumbler, footed, 4"	— —	— —	— —	3.50
Water set, 7 piece	46.00	— —	— —	— —

MACBETH-EVANS GLASS COMPANY

AMERICAN SWEETHEART	PINK	WHITE
Bowl, oval, 11"	11.25 – 18.75	30.00 – 47.50
Creamer, footed	3.25 – 7.25	3.25 – 8.25
Cup and saucer	7.00 – 9.00	7.25 – 12.25
Plate, 9"	4.75	4.25 – 9.00
Plate, chop	— —	10.00
Platter, oval, 13"	10.25 – 28.00	25.50 – 41.00
Salt and pepper	140.00 – 160.00	142.00 – 205.00
Soup, cream	8.75 – 16.75	30.00
Sugar, open	5.75	3.25 – 8.25
Tumbler, 4½"	23.00	— —

DOGWOOD	PINK	GREEN	WHITE	CRYSTAL
Bowl, 5½"	5.25– 12.25	— —	— —	— —
Cup and saucer	4.25– 8.75	15.25– 17.75	— —	6.25
Luncheon set, 3 piece	— —	19.50	— —	— —
Plate, 8"	1.75– 5.75	1.75– 6.75	— —	2.00
Plate, 12"	8.25– 15.50	— —	26.00– 31.00	— —
Plate, grill, 10½"	6.00– 9.50	5.25– 8.25	— —	— —
Sugar and creamer	9.50	52.00	— —	— —
Tumbler, 4"	15.50	10.50	— —	5.25
Whiskey	— —	4.25	— —	— —

PETALWARE	PINK	RED	WHITE	CRYSTAL
Bowl, 5¾"	3.25 – 5.25	— —	3.00 – 4.00	— —
Cup	2.50 – 4.00	2.50	2.75 – 5.00	4.25
Plate, 8"	1.75 – 3.00	— —	2.75	2.75 – 4.00
Platter, oval, 13"	4.75 – 6.75	— —	10.25 – 15.00	3.00
Saucer	1.50	— —	1.25 – 3.75	1.75
Sherbet, low, footed	2.25 – 3.75	— —	3.75	— —
Sugar and creamer	8.25	— —	6.25 – 12.00	6.25

S PATTERN	AMBER	CRYSTAL
Bowl, 5½"	2.25 – 3.75	— —
Creamer	3.25	3.00
Cup and saucer	2.75 – 5.75	3.50
Plate, 6"	2.00	1.50

	PINK	GREEN
Plate, 9¼"	2.75 – 6.50	2.75
Sherbet, low, footed	2.75 – 4.75	4.25
Sugar	3.25	2.75
Tumbler, 3½"	4.00	3.75

THISTLE	PINK	GREEN
Bowl, 5½"	8.75 – 10.50	11.00
Cup	8.50	— —
Luncheon set, 3 piece	— —	21.00
Plate, 8"	7.75	— —
Saucer	3.25	3.50

Glossary
of
Depression
Glass Terms

ACID-ETCHED PROCESS: Design cut into mold with acid. Produces glassware with decorations in relief, looks etched, but does not need hand-finishing.

ART DECO: Name of pervasive decorative art style of 1920s and 1930s. Characterized by bold outlines, streamlined and rectilinear forms, and use of new materials.

BEVERAGE SET: Pitcher and set of tumblers for serving drinks.

BUTTER DISH: Table: Plate, usually six inches round, with dome-shaped lid. Refrigerator: Plate with lid, usually oblong, for storing one-pound bars of butter.

CANDY JAR: Often made as part of dinnerware set. Usually footed and stemmed, for serving sweets.

CARNIVAL: Iridized glassware popular during the early 20th century.

CHIGGER BITE: Term used by auctioneers to describe small chip in a dish.

CHIPPED-MOLD PROCESS: Process of cutting design directly into mold by use of tools. Produced intricate flat patterns, but less complicated designs than produced by mold-etched process. Does not appear etched.

CHUNKED: Badly damaged.

COASTER: Round, flat disk, used under drinking glass, occasionally used as ashtray.

COLOR: Depression glass was made in a wide variety of colors. See list at end of glossary.

COMPORT: Dish with stem and foot for serving desserts. Also called compote or compotier.

CRACKER JAR: Cookie jar, usually sold with product packed inside.

CRACKLEWARE: Popular pattern of 1920s and 1930s. Crackled effect achieved by surface decoration in mold.

CREAM SOUP DISH: Bowl, usually five inches in diameter with two handles on opposite sides of the rim.

CUT-MOLD PROCESS: Old process used during the Depression to make glassware which resembled cut glass. Because of poor quality of glass, this glass lacks brilliance of earlier pressed glass.

DINNER SET: Complete table sets usually sold as services for four, six, eight or twelve. Each set included dinner plates (usually nine inch), plates for serving fruit, soup bowls, dessert plates and tumblers for beverages. Sets frequently included serving plates, coasters, ashtrays, candleholders, sugar and creamer sets, salt and pepper sets, grill plates, candy jars, cookie jars, and butter dishes. Often given as premiums.

FIRED-ON: Color applied and baked on at factory.

FLASHED-ON: Color added over crystal, tends to wear off with use.

FROSTED GLASS: Glass which has been sprayed with acid to produce translucent appearance.

GLASSBAKE: Name used by McKee Glass Company for a line of cookware, children's sets, and fish sets. Occasionally decorated with green.

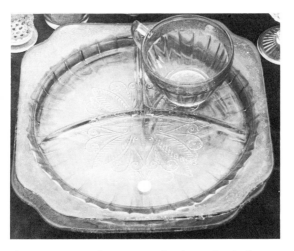

GRILL PLATE: Dinner-sized plate divided into three sections.

ICE LIP: Lip of beverage pitcher that is folded inward to catch ice cubes when pouring. Lip formed by hand with tools.

LUNCHEON SET: Table service that does not include plates over eight inches and has fewer pieces than dinner sets.

MAYONNAISE: Open, cone-shaped compote.

MOLD-ETCHED PROCESS: Pattern cut into mold by series of wax transfers and acid baths. Produces glassware that appears etched or incised but which has raised pattern with etched surface. Glass made from these molds can be identified by the raised design. Most collectible Depression glassware decorated by this process.

NAPPY: Fashionable term of 1930s for round or oval dish with flat bottom and sloping sides. Made in various sizes, for fruit, soup, cereal, salad.

NITE SET: Two-piece set consisting of tumbler which sits inverted on jug (jug usually without handle).

OATMEAL GLASS: Refers to "Sandwich" or other patterned glass used as premiums in boxes of oatmeal.

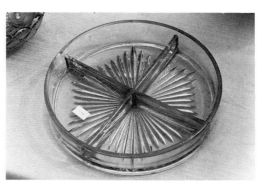

OPEN STOCK: Items that were sold individually as well as in sets.

PASTE-MOLD PROCESS: Process which produces polished effect on glass surface. Because it is expensive, it was seldom used on Depression glass.

PITCHER: Also called jug, ball jug, tilt jug.

POT GLASS: Glass which is melted in open or covered pots in furnace. Often contains different colors.

PREMIUMS: Glassware used as promotional items or giveaways by businesses.

PRESSED-MOLD PROCESS: Mold shaped around wood model. Produces glass without embellishment or polished effect.

PYREX: Trademark name for heat-resistant glassware made by Corning for cooking. Now misused to describe all heat-resistant glassware for home.

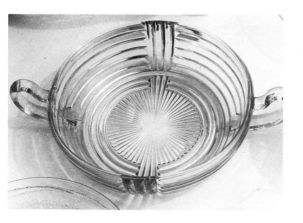

RAYED: Having a spoke-like design on bottom (found on some glassware).

REAMER: Dish with ridged dome in center for extracting juice from citrus fruit.

REFRIGERATOR WARE: Dishes, most often with covers, for storing food in refrigerator. Often made in bright colors and in stackable sets.

RUBY FLASHED: Subjected to Federal Glass Company process that covered surface of clear glass with red coating.

SALAD SET: One large bowl and six or more nappies. Sets frequently included plates.

SALVER: Large serving plate. Also called chop plate.

SATIN FINISH: Cloudy or frosted translucence produced by acid-etched process.

TID-BIT: Two- or three-tiered serving dish made of increasingly smaller plates connected by metal pole in center. Usually 12 to 15 inches tall.

Color Glossary

AMBER: Golden Glow (Federal), Topaz (Hocking).

BLUE-GREEN: Ultra-marine (Jeannette).

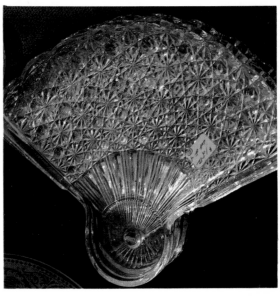

CLEAR: Crystal (all manufacturers).

CREAM OPAQUE: Clambroth, Cremax and Chinex (Macbeth-Evans, now Corning). Chinex often made with pale brown edges and decorated with flowers or castles, sometimes made with pink edges and floral pattern.

DEEP BLUE: Ritz Blue (Macbeth-Evans), Cobalt, Dark Blue, Deep Blue.

GREEN: Springtime Green (Federal), Emerald (Hocking), Imperial Green (Imperial).

IVORY: Ivrene (Macbeth-Evans), Ivory (McKee).

MEDIUM BLUE: Madonna (Federal).

OPAQUE BLACK: Black, Ebony. Black glass seldom made during the Depression.

OPAQUE BLUE: Delphite (Jeannette), Poudre Blue (McKee). Sometimes incorrectly referred to as "blue milk glass."

OPAQUE GREEN: Jadite or Jad-ite (Jeannette), Jade Green (McKee), Jade-ite (Hocking).

OPAQUE WHITE: Milk White, Monax (Macbeth-Evans), Platonite (Hazel Atlas). Sometimes made with fired-on colors.

PINK: Rose, Rose Marie (Imperial), Rose Pink, Rose Tint, Rose Glow (Federal), Nu-Rose, Wild Rose (Macbeth-Evans), Flamingo (Hocking).

PURPLE: Burgundy (Hazel Atlas), Amethyst.

RED: Royal Ruby (Hocking), Ruby Red (Macbeth-Evans).

YELLOW: Vaseline.